D1318548

AB5500 370056

David Paige
Behind the Scenes at the Aquarium
Photographs Roger Ruhlin

KEEP
HANDS
OUT
OF ALL TANKS

ALBERT WHITMAN & Company, Chicago

The author and photographer especially appreciate the assistance and courtesies extended to them by Director William P. Braker and his staff at the John G. Shedd Aquarium of Chicago. Their work enriches the appreciation of the natural world, provides information, and furthers research.

Library of Congress Cataloging in Publication Data

Paige, David
  Behind the scenes at the aquarium.

  SUMMARY: Photographs and text present the challenge of caring for fish and other water animals in a large city aquarium.
    1. Aquariums, Public—Juvenile literature.
  [1. Aquariums] I. Ruhlin, Roger. II. Title.
  QL78.P32   639'.34   77-24670
  ISBN 0-8075-0607-9

Contents

PART ONE:
Aquarium World

Is that a smile on Chico's face?   *5*
What an aquarium is,   *6*
Aquariums, old and new,   *8*
Many kinds of life on exhibit,   *9*
All aboard for a collecting trip,   *11*
How specimens are taken,   *13*
Collecting can mean adventure,   *14*
Specimens from ship to shore,   *16*
Gifts to aquariums,   *18*
A jeep and a turtle,   *19*
Endangered and unusual species,   *20*

PART TWO:
Water Habitats

The aquarium challenge,   *23*
Miles of pipes,   *24*
Guarding life in the aquarium,   *26*
Oceanariums have an advantage,   *26*
Making exhibits meaningful,   *27*

PART THREE:
The Workers

What you don't see,   *33*
The director knows fish—and people,   *33*
Departments and workers,   *34*
Fishes and aquarists,   *35*
Special assignments,   *36*
Care and feeding,   *38*
Health is important,   *40*
Contributing to science,   *42*
Microscopes, films, and books,   *43*
Making the aquarium known,   *45*
Still other workers,   *46*
An aquarium is more than fish,   *46*

Glossary,   *47*
Index,   *48*

Aquarium World

■

An aquarium is the place to meet the wonderful world of water and water animals, a world where humans are not at home.

Is that a smile on Chico's face?

His name is Chico, and he was born in Brazil, in the Amazon River. At birth he wriggled backward into the world, tail first, because he is an air-breathing animal, a mammal and not a fish. If he had been born headfirst, he might well have drowned.

For more than fourteen years, the John G. Shedd Aquarium, in Chicago, has been Chico's home. He's a favorite with visitors and aquarists, the keepers who work behind the scenes at the aquarium.

Chico is a freshwater dolphin, and this means he's a very unusual animal. He is related to the more familiar marine dolphins which live in oceans and seas and sometimes explore river mouths. The marine dolphins are the ones most often seen performing graceful leaps and amusing tricks.

What makes Chico of special interest is how he differs from other dolphins. He is a primitive, or very early, form of dolphin.

Like all members of his species, Chico is descended from land mammals. The bristly hairs on his beaklike snout are a reminder that he is a mammal, because all mammals have hair. When he was born, he drank his mother's milk.

The fin on his back is poorly developed, not like the graceful sail of the bottle-nosed dolphin. His flippers look like hands covered with waterproof upholstery, the fingers webbed together. In fact, with his pinkish-gray coloring, Chico looks like a giant water toy, a toy weighing 220 pounds.

His eyes are small, and his vision is probably poor if compared to that of a saltwater dolphin. But this would not have been a handicap in his original muddy, river-bottom world. Like all dolphins, he sends out sound waves through the water and uses their echoes to find food and avoid swimming into obstacles.

←

Behind the scenes, Chico, an Amazon River dolphin, seeks attention from a volunteer worker at the aquarium. Here you can see the blowhole through which he breathes.

No one's too young—or too old—to find an aquarium a fascinating place to visit.

Watching Chico move lazily around his tank leads some visitors to think he should have companionship. Here again he is different from his marine relatives, who swim in schools. Even if he were free, Chico could probably live alone, although he might also belong to a small group of other dolphins.

Chico likes to play and has learned some tricks. Intelligent and friendly, he likes to be petted by his aquarist, or keeper. Because of the permanent shape of his lips he always appears to be smiling.

He has learned to trust humans and tell one from another. As an experiment, several aquarists, dressed alike, stood near the rim of Chico's tank. To which one did he swim? Without hesitating, he chose the man who over the years fed, petted, and cared for him. Chico was not to be fooled.

What an aquarium is

Chico's story tells a lot about what an aquarium is and why it is important.

An aquarium is an artificial home for living water animals and plants. It can be a goldfish bowl of your own or a public building for the exhibition of aquatic life.

An oceanarium is a saltwater aquarium with outdoor tanks often big enough to hold a whale and with other tanks built to exhibit many different fish living together, much as they would be found in the ocean. Shows featuring performing marine animals, such as dolphins, are popular at oceanariums.

Aquariums and oceanariums try to duplicate the natural surroundings, or habitat, of the animals they display. Walking along a dim aquarium gallery, you can see the fish swimming in the sunlight, sometimes so close to the window side of the tank that only the glass and a little water separate you from them. At an oceanarium, you can peer through porthole-like windows set at different depths in the side of a huge outdoor tank. The underwater wonders you see are fascinating to watch.

Aquariums are more than entertainment, however. They are places for study and research, too.

Chico's story also introduces the people, most of them well out of sight, who care for the fish and other animals. Zoos have keepers, but aquariums have aquarists who feed, handle, and look after the animals in their charge.

The great difference between a zoo and an aquarium is the environment needed for life. Most mammals, birds, reptiles, and other zoo animals are like man: they live in what is sometimes called "an ocean of air." Fish, shellfish and lobsters, mammals like dolphins, sea birds such as penguins, and creatures like sponges all must live in or near water. For some it is salt water,

Chico lifts himself out of the water to take food from Senior Aquarist Howard Karsner's hand at the Shedd Aquarium, Chicago. Small teeth line the dolphin's smiling jaws. What looks somewhat like Chico's forehead is the sense organ called a melon. It sends out sonarlike signals the dolphin uses to avoid obstacles.

A view of the Seaquarium at Miami, taken from a plane, shows a variety of tanks built to hold different kinds of sea life. The mild Florida climate makes such outdoor tanks possible.

like that of the ocean; for others it is fresh water, free of salt, like that found in rivers and inland lakes.

Aquariums, old and new

In ancient Rome 2,000 years ago there were outdoor and indoor ponds where different fish were displayed. These early aquariums were for entertainment, but they also led to some understanding of how fish live.

In ancient China, too, aquariums were popular. Some fish were raised as pets. The most famous were the goldfish, a kind of carp, bred for beauty and color.

During the 1800s, large aquariums were built in many European cities.

When wars were fought, most of these aquariums were destroyed or closed. Today there are aquariums in many European and Asian cities. Among outstanding ones you may some day visit are those at Copenhagen, in Denmark; Bergen, in Norway; Stuttgart and Cologne, in West Germany; and Amsterdam, in The Netherlands. Tokyo and Kobe, Japanese cities, have fine aquariums, and so does Hong Kong.

In the United States, aquarium building also began in the 1800s. The National Aquarium, now in Washington, D.C., was opened at Woods Hole, Massachusetts, in 1873. But most of the American collections famous today were built after 1900.

The largest aquarium under one roof is the John G. Shedd Aquarium, opened in Chicago in 1930. The New York Aquarium dates from 1896, but its present quarters are new. The New England Aquarium, Boston, the Steinhart in San Francisco, and the Aquarium of Niagara Falls are all important. Many other cities also have valuable collections. In Canada, Vancouver is well known for its aquarium.

Oceanariums include Marineland of Florida at St. Augustine; Seaquarium at Miami, a pioneer in this type of aquarium; Sea World at San Diego; and among the largest, Marineland of the Pacific, at Palos Verdes Estates, California.

Many kinds of life on exhibit

Fish shown at aquariums come from all the oceans, even the Arctic, and from seas, lakes, rivers, small streams, marshes, and ponds. In specialized collections, exhibits are chosen to highlight certain interests, for example, freshwa-

The yellow-tailed clownfish, about 3½ inches long, is from the Indian Ocean. The sea anemones in the same exhibit look like flowers but are water animals related to corals and jellyfish.

ter fish native to the area where the aquarium is built.

An aquarium like the Shedd has at one time about 4,500 fishes, belonging to over 500 species.

Aquariums are not limited to fish. Other marine life is on display. Beautiful sea anemones look like flowers but are really animals. There are lobsters, crabs, starfish, sea horses, sea cucumbers, octopuses, eels, squids, mussels, clams, oysters, and much more.

Mammals from the sea are included, too. Seals, walruses, dolphins, otters, and if there is enough room, as in an oceanarium, whales and large sharks. Some aquariums have sea turtles, sea snakes, alligators, and crocodiles. They may also exhibit such water birds as penguins.

While some fish and many turtles are long lived, most sea animals have short lives. Replacement can be a problem because it is not easy in captivity to

This spiny lobster measures about a foot across. It is a scavenger from the Caribbean Sea and digs into the gravel for shellfish and worms.

Here are two freshwater fish familiar to Midwestern anglers. The young hybrid northern pike and muskie is about 10 inches long. The common blue gill is about two-thirds as large. Water plants give this display the look of a streambed.

breed some of the most-wanted aquarium fish. So, while zoos are able to supply new animals by setting up breeding programs, aquariums must find other ways to fill out their collections. True, some specimens are traded, and some can be bought from commercial dealers; others come through the cooperation of government agencies. But these different ways do not fill all an aquarium's needs. The staff takes an active part in collecting what is to be exhibited.

All aboard for a collecting trip

Some of the most exciting behind-the-scenes work actually happens far from the aquarium. It can be in the Caribbean Sea, at a nearby river, in a salt marsh, or faraway in the South Pacific or the South Seas.

This business of collecting is not easy, because sea life ranges from fish of tiny size to 15-foot whales weighing tons.

Who goes on collecting expeditions? The director, who heads the aquarium and is a science specialist, often goes, as do the curators, who are also trained in biology and zoology.

The crew is likely to include aquarists, trained as deep-sea divers. Sometimes there are students and a few guests who are lucky enough to be invited. Everyone must be able to swim and dive.

Planning comes first. Will most of the specimens be found in warm waters near the Florida Keys? Is the goal more distant—Hawaii or some more far-off Pacific islands? Or perhaps the site is a nearby river, lake, or swamp.

Boats are especially designed for collecting. Unlike ordinary fishing boats, these have water-filled tanks to hold live fish. The water is kept at a suitable temperature and circulates all the time, driven by pumps. This circulation keeps oxygen in the water to supply the fishes' needs.

Fish, even sharks, are surprisingly delicate. Nothing is worse than to have a fish die before it is even removed from

Plans for a Shedd Aquarium project are shared by Director William P. Braker and Curator of Fishes Don Zumwalt. On the office wall is a mounted sailfish.

Aboard the Shedd Aquarium's collecting boat, *Coral Reef*, specimens are emptied from a trap to a water-filled tub.

the collecting boat. Here's where know-how and experience make a difference.

How specimens are taken

Fish are caught in different ways. Some can be netted as the collector wades through shallow water.

For others, nothing more than a hook and line are needed, as in fishing you may have done from a dock or boat. Bait to attract the fish is put on a barbless hook and the line cast into the water. The fish snaps at the bait, and (if the aquarist is lucky) the fish is reeled in.

Quickly unhooked and dropped into a bucket or holding tank, the fish is in good shape except for a cut lip.

Another way to collect fish is one used by commercial fishermen. Large nets are trailed through the water behind the boat. When the nets fill with a catch, they are hauled aboard. The specimens to be saved are quickly culled, or sorted, from the wriggling mass and dropped into tanks.

One commercial collector has his boat equipped with a dredge which is

That's a slurp gun Don Zumwalt holds. You can see how the piston draws fish into the plastic tube. Nearby are hand nets and a sturdy underwater collecting cage.

dragged over the sea bottom. If the floor is sandy, there may be hermit crabs, sand dollars, and starfish. If the bottom is rocky, then other kinds of specimens, such as small shrimp and even little octopuses may be spilled on the deck.

Many specimens are not collected by fishing but by diving. Swimmers with scuba gear—rubber suits called wet suits, flippers, masks, and compressed-air tanks—leave the boat to search for fish and sea life.

Sometimes the divers set traps on the sea floor or near coral formations. Later, they return to see what their traps hold.

Hand nets, too, are of help, and divers use them to snare fish as they swim past.

How many specimens can one expedition bring back? Perhaps 300 to more than 600, although these specimens do not all belong to separate kinds, or species.

Collecting can mean adventure

The underwater world is a silent one full of startling shapes and color. It holds surprises and dangers.

Fishes hide among rocks in coral and even in the wrecks of sunken ships. To catch fish a diver can't reach, an anesthetic is handy. Squeezed from a plastic bottle into an underwater cave, the anesthetic numbs the fish. They float from their hiding place and are easily caught.

For some hard-to-catch small fish, the slurp gun is the answer. "Gun" is not really a good name for this device, because it does not shoot anything out. Instead, the slurp gun sucks in something—a fish. The diver aims the gun into a hole under a rock and slurp! a fish is drawn into the gun's tube.

Jagged rocks and sharp coral can cause deep wounds. The possibility of dangerous fish like sharks and barracudas keeps divers alert. Any failure in equipment is a hazard, and even the weather can cause trouble.

Once four Shedd Aquarium divers were exploring a shipwreck not much below the water's surface. Above them, standing by, was the 75-foot boat owned by the aquarium, the *Coral Reef.*

Suddenly a storm darkened the Caribbean sky. With incredible swiftness,

Captain Dave Bakara, standing on the top deck, commands the collecting boat. Note the spotlights, nets, and stern platform among other items of special equipment. *Courtesy of John G. Shedd Aquarium*

With great care, workers at the Miami Seaquarium move a marine dolphin, making sure it will not be injured.

winds roared over the water, and waves tossed the *Coral Reef* toward the shipwreck. The divers' lives were in peril, and the boat and its crew in danger.

While the captain kept the *Coral Reef* away from the wreckage, the aquarium's director, William Braker, set out in a small motorized lifeboat. With a combination of seamanship and a good share of luck, he reached the four divers and pulled them aboard. Safe on the expedition's boat, they all agreed that this was an experience not to be forgotten.

There are other memories of a different kind, to be recalled with wonder. At night, bright lights are rigged to hang over the water around the *Coral Reef*. The sea comes alive as fish are attracted to the light. Stars shine overhead in the dark sky and the jewel-like fish leap—it is the sort of experience that happens only a few times, and not for many people.

Specimens from ship to shore

Big fish eat little fish. Such fish are part of a food chain which may start with plankton, the almost microscopic plants and animals floating in the ocean.

The small plankton-eating fish are gobbled by larger fish, which in turn may make a meal for even bigger fish. In some species, fish behave like cannibals and eat their own kind.

All this means that fish taken on a day of diving, netting, fishing, or dredging cannot be thrown into a single holding tank. They have to be sorted and separated—or forty different small fish may be reduced to five large fish by the time port is reached.

When the collecting boat docks, the next part of the work begins. Because sea life is delicate, it is more likely to survive and arrive at the aquarium in good condition if it is shipped as quickly as possible.

In the past, fish were sent by train or truck. The Shedd Aquarium owned a railroad car, named "Nautilus," which was fitted with tanks to hold live fish and with sleeping quarters for staff members. The trip from the Gulf coast to Chicago took two days.

Now it is more efficient to send fish by air. Specimens are packed in water-filled plastic bags and put in Styrofoam containers. Within hours instead of days, the journey from sea to aquarium is completed. Staff members still travel with shipments to guard against mishaps.

Swimming and diving are required of all the crew on a collecting trip. Here you can see some of the scuba equipment used in coral reef diving.
Courtesy of John G. Shedd Aquarium

Gifts to aquariums

Aquariums, like zoos, have animals given to them. Sometimes these are pets which have outgrown home care and which may or may not be suitable for a collection. There are unusual donations, too.

When the Chicago aquarium opened in 1930, some of the men who had worked on the construction of the building went to a local fish market. They bought live carp and brought them back to help stock the large central pool, a featured exhibit area.

Not so long ago, a mischance resulted in an unexpected gift of sharks. A stunt rider planned to leap his motorcycle over a tank of hungry sharks. Fortunately for the sharks, and perhaps for the stunt man, the leap never took place, prevented by an accident. Three of the sharks became aquarium property.

Another source of donations is the Fish and Wildlife Service. This United States government agency enforces the Endangered Species Conservation Act. The service takes over shipments of animals not permitted for sale in this country. Baby sea turtles are sometimes found in illegal shipments. Since these turtles belong to an endangered species, they are boarded at an aquarium. They are raised there until they are large enough to be released in the ocean.

Turtles may lumber along on the land, but in water they swim quickly and easily. They are the only reptiles with shells, and all turtles, even sea turtles, lay their eggs on land.

A jeep and a turtle

The story of a 400-pound gift turtle is told by Craig Phillips in his book about the building of the Miami Seaquarium.

The adventure began when an aquarium operator offered a large female loggerhead turtle to the Seaquarium—if someone would get it.

This sea turtle is interesting because its throat tissue can absorb oxygen from water. When the turtle is active, it must rise regularly to the surface to breathe air into its lungs. But when it is motionless it can rest on the ocean floor for long periods at a time.

In a borrowed jeep, with a mattress and pillow in the back, Craig Phillips set out on an eventful ride. After a drive of 200 miles he arrived, ready to claim the turtle.

With the help of six men, he got the huge animal on its back and into the jeep. To make his unusual passenger comfortable, he covered it with a blanket to prevent its skin from drying out. He pushed the pillow under the turtle's head and was about to leave when the first crisis came.

The turtle began to move about violently and tore at the jeep's interior with its claws. Borrowing a hacksaw, Mr. Phillips became a turtle manicurist and trimmed the sharp claw tips.

As long as the jeep moved, all was well. But engine trouble set in, and

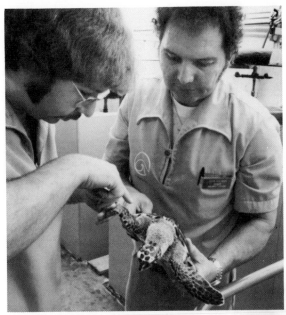

The hawksbill turtle being examined by aquarist Dan Christopher is held by head diver John Kolman. He can appreciate this turtle's swimming ability.

stops and starts became frequent. This made the turtle restless, and once it sent its blanket flying out of the jeep. The return trip began to seem endless.

Even when all was quiet there was no way to ignore the turtle. Twice a minute it sighed deeply and breathed heavily. And no animal, reports Mr. Phillips, has worse-smelling breath than a loggerhead.

The jeep had to be repaired, so when a dinner break came, Mr. Phillips stopped at a service station. When he returned after his meal, two very suspicious garagemen eyed him. The sighs coming from the blanket-covered body sounded as if someone were dying. Pulling back

Humboldt penguins wait in a holding tank until a home can be found for them. Note the warning sign.

steps are taken to save them. Other species are not as yet threatened but for other reasons are of special interest.

The Australian lungfish is not endangered, but it is a rare kind of animal and a valuable aquarium exhibit. It's unusual because it has both gills and lungs and thus can live in water or on land.

Maybe you think all penguins live in a cold climate, at home on snow and ice. Humboldt penguins, natives of Peru, are quite different. The Antarctic would be a very unfriendly place for them.

As in the case of many endangered or unusual animals, aquarium people would like to breed Humboldt penguins to enlarge exhibits. But this is not such an easy project.

For some time the Shedd Aquarium had a pair of these South American birds. Some eggs were laid, but perhaps because the shells were weak, the eggs always broke. The curator thought that if the aquarium had a larger flock, the chances of breeding and raising young might be improved.

Male and female penguins look exactly alike. With six penguins, at least one pair of male and female birds is likely, so the Shedd curator bought four new Humboldt penguins.

Two of the penguins lived only a short time. The remaining two were introduced to the pair already used to life at the Shedd Aquarium. Trouble! The old

the blanket, Mr. Phillips showed the men one of the most astonishing passengers they'd ever seen.

Endangered and unusual species

Certain species of animals and plants are endangered and may disappear if no birds attacked the newcomers and there was nothing to do but separate them. The young birds were put in a holding tank in a work area closed to visitors. There the penguins waited while the curator tried to find a collection where the two outcast birds could be boarded.

Temporarily, at least, the hope of having penguin chicks was abandoned. The 14-year-old penguins had kept their territory at the Shedd for their own.

Endangered sea turtles are another story. Overhunting has nearly wiped them out, but these turtles thrive in captivity. They have huge appetites and are extremely unfussy about what they'll eat. The problem is their rapid growth. They can all too quickly eat themselves out of a welcome.

The Shedd had four such turtles, a loggerhead, a hawksbill, and two green turtles, weighing from 60 to more than 120 pounds apiece. Could these turtles survive if set free in their natural environment?

The turtles were tagged and flown to Florida for release. Nine months later one was captured, its tag noted, and freed. Here was proof an aquarium-raised turtle could live on its own.

The queen triggerfish is a tropical fish about 16 inches long. Triggerfish have several unusual features, including bodies covered by platelike scales. Their teeth are strong and sharp enough to break off coral in search for food.

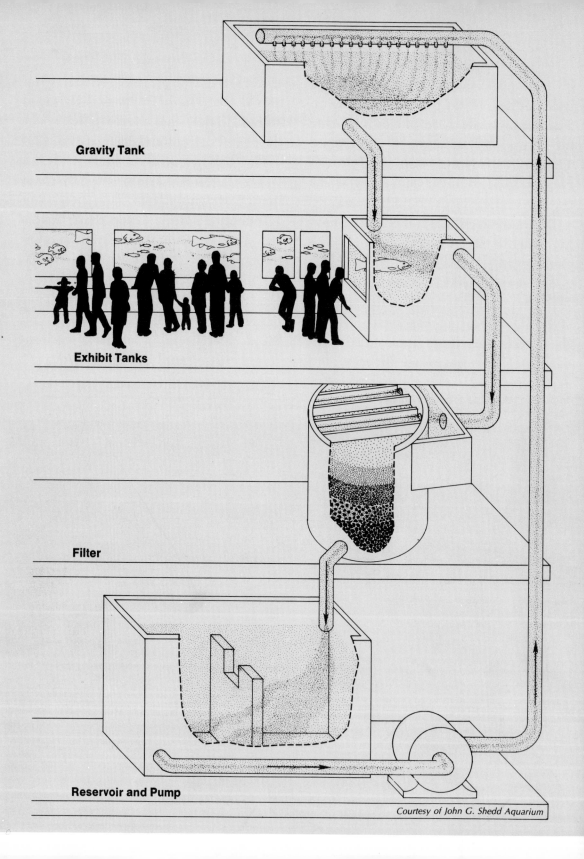

Gravity Tank

Exhibit Tanks

Filter

Reservoir and Pump

Courtesy of John G. Shedd Aquarium

Water Habitats

■■

Imagine a living Earth museum far out in space, complete with air, soil, water, plants and animals in natural settings. To build such a museum would be much like setting up an aquarium that duplicates the water world found in nature.

The aquarium challenge

When you visit an aquarium or oceanarium you see an assortment of creatures, most strange, some familiar, some rare. They are all alike in one way: they depend for life upon the aquarium and its staff.

You may not think of this as you watch a rainbow trout swim in what looks like a cool, shaded stream. The bright-colored clownfish in another tank hovers near the anemone, unafraid of its poisonous tentacles which keep other fish away.

Turtles splash and swim gracefully. On land, they are clumsy, but in water they move with smooth speed.

There is the lion fish, as odd and beautiful as it is dangerous. The quill-like spines on its body have a poison which is extremely painful to humans.

Hundreds of fish, plus crabs and lobsters, sea horses and dolphins, seals and penguins—how can an aquarium house all these?

It's obvious that water, in huge quantities, is essential for everything living in the displays. And water is heavy, as you know if you've tried to move a home fish tank or carry a bucket of water.

Providing huge quantities of water is only one part of the problem. There must be fresh water and salt water. For tropical fish, the water must be warm; for specimens from cold climates, water must be chilled to a point not far from freezing. Other fish need temperatures between these extremes.

← This diagram of the water system in an aquarium shows how pumps and gravity keep water constantly moving through tanks, pipes, filters, and reservoirs.

23

Once, inland aquariums depended upon ocean salt water, shipped in from seacoasts by barge or railroad tank car. Now there are chemical formulas for mixing salt water from fresh water by adding the right amounts of salt and other minerals.

If fish are to stay alive and healthy, the water they swim in must have enough oxygen and be free of wastes and impurities. This is why water in an aquarium is always filtered and never still, but always in circulation.

Miles of pipes

Miles of pipes, pumps, heaters, cooling units, and filters are all built into complicated systems. This is the domain of the workers in an aquarium's Mainte-nance Department. Day after day, engineers and workers keep these systems operating.

At the Shedd, 75 miles of pipes carry water from fish tanks through filters to reservoirs on a lower level. Pumps send the water up to overhead tanks, where it is aerated to add oxygen. From there the water again makes its circular journey throughout exhibit and reserve tanks. Seven separate systems are used, three for fresh water, four for salt water.

Once when part of the freshwater system was shut down for repairs, a wholly unexpected discovery called for detective work.

The basement reservoir, which holds 300,000 gallons of water, contained live

The sign above the lion fish means what it says. Poison from the tips of this fish's sharp spines causes extreme pain.

Identifying colors and markings tell the aquarium engineers and maintenance workers the purpose of different pipes.

fish! A colony of African cichlids, a small freshwater fish, were swimming in the enormous tank.

Since water is filtered before entering the reservoir, it was hard to explain the mystery. The fish were certainly too large to have swum through the filters. The answer seemed to be that fish eggs, spawned in the cichlid exhibit tank, were small enough to pass through the filtering bypass system. Somehow, the eggs had hatched in the reservoir.

This was amazing, but the next discovery was even more so. A dead fish, neatly cut in half, was found floating on top of the water in the reservoir. Could some other, larger fish be lurking there?

Indeed there was—nothing less than a good-sized piranha, a South American freshwater fish, famous for its appetite and sharp teeth.

The curator remembered that some time earlier there had been piranha young, or larvae, in the aquarium. Some of these larvae must also have gone through the filter bypass. One fish had the good luck to find the cichlids, a ready-made food supply.

Water constantly flowing in and out of the holding tank is as necessary as food for the health of these cichlids, a Central American species.

Guarding life in the aquarium

This all seemed hard to believe, but the curators could find no other theory to fit the facts.

Maintenance engineers are on duty, day and night. If the electricity which powers the pumps, the heating and cooling machinery, and the control equipment should fail, many fish and much of the sea life would be unable to live long. Many, in fact, would die within an hour. Engineers therefore have emergency standby sources of power to prevent such a disaster.

All the pumps and support systems operate from a control center. Some centers are controlled by computers which set off an alarm when any part of the system does not work as it should.

In a large aquarium, thousands of gallons of water are pumped a minute. As much as several million gallons are used in the whole operation.

At the Shedd Aquarium, the water system is a closed one. This means that the same water is circulated over and over. Special reservoirs hold water for aging and to meet emergencies. New salt water is added only about twice a year, but fresh water, from Lake Michigan, is added all the time in small batches.

Oceanariums have an advantage

The amount of water used by aquariums is increasing as designs change. Once, small display tanks were preferred.

26

Now huge tanks which mix many kinds of fish, living at different depths, are popular. Such oceanarium tanks come close to showing what a natural water environment is like.

Oceanariums are almost always located near a large body of salt water. Most are built where the climate is mild, and the best known are in Florida and California.

Because all their exhibits are not under one roof, oceanariums feature tanks of immense size. Ocean water, filtered, is sometimes pumped directly into the water systems.

The largest oceanarium tank is at Marineland of the Pacific, in southern California. It holds 540,000 gallons of water, about five or six times as much as any indoor tank. Here more than 3,000 fish are kept: sharks, rays, sawfish, tarpons, giant sea turtles, and many smaller fish. In size, the fish range from those not much bigger than a fist to a giant grouper, or sea bass, which weighs 400 pounds.

Making exhibits meaningful

Sea life comes in a variety of shapes, colors, sizes, beauty, and even ugliness. Each tank holds a surprise.

The control panel for the main filtration center at the Shedd Aquarium is checked by Dennis Kucharski of the Maintenance Department. Warning signals call for action.

Eels look like snakes but are fish, not reptiles. Moray eels, some more than 5 feet long, are found in coral reef waters.

hide-and-seek with watchers on the other side of the glass partition.

Making displays meaningful and beautiful is hard, interesting work for the exhibit designers. They must cope with showing off a tiny tropical fish and

This habitat for a harbor seal is built of skillfully made plastic casts, as you can see if you look closely.

As you enjoy watching the fish you can learn something about them, too. The men and women in the Exhibits Department of the aquarium are happy if you are entertained and educated at the same time. They have planned ways to catch your interest and give you information.

As much as possible, displays are designed to show the kind of home a fish would naturally have. Fish that live in the same environment are placed together. Anemones, starfishes, and sea urchins may also be included, and plants, too, if they are appropriate.

A good display is a lot like a stageset. The eel's tank is an example of one similar to the fish's natural environment. It lets the eel hide among rocks and glide in and out of passageways. The eel is unaware it appears to play planning a background for a fish as big as the 450-pound jewfish.

A lot of planning goes on before any tank is set up. Designers build small-scale models. Before the exhibit itself is begun, aquarists test materials to learn whether they are safe and durable.

Accuracy is important. Designers often take photographs—of a coral reef or a mountain stream, for example—to make sure even small details are right.

Workers have three guides in mind as they plan tank interiors. First, the natural behavior of the fish or animal must be encouraged. Second, the tank must look attractive and be easy to keep clean. And last, and perhaps most important, nothing should endanger fish or aquarists.

Exhibit workers, called "zibbets" at the Shedd Aquarium, have to know the inhabitants of each tank. They know a shy fish needs hiding places and large fish can't be squeezed into a small tank.

Real rocks, shells, and living plants are fine in some tanks, but pose problems in others. Suppose a large exhibit, such as the one for the seals, is meant to suggest a rocky coast. Does that mean tons of rocks?

When live materials are used, aquarists put the finishing touches on habitats. Here, Howard Karsner is positioning plants in the exhibit which will hold the Australian lungfish.

The zibbets people have found an answer. It is "no." Plastic casts are made of rock formations. Plants and corals, too, can be reproduced in this way. Because the casts are like molds and hollow, they are easier to move and put in place than real rocks would be.

Sometimes zibbets solve one problem and run into others. What looks lifelike in planning stages may look all wrong in water. Materials after being in water for a while may become too brittle or too soft. Then zibbets hunt for substitutes.

If the zibbets do their work well, no one guesses the rocks on which the penguins perch are not real. Only the workers behind the scenes know the artful construction involved.

The Coral Reef exhibit at the Shedd Aquarium challenged the Exhibits Department and the curators. This large circular tank reproduces a Florida reef and features the life found there.

To install living coral was impossible because growing conditions could not be duplicated in the exhibit tank. Coral formations not containing living animals rather quickly disintegrated.

Using a scale model of the Coral Reef exhibit at the Shedd Aquarium, Curator of Exhibits Emanuel Ledecky-Janecek and Sally Davidson, exhibits designer, experiment with how the diver will look among the rocks and corals.

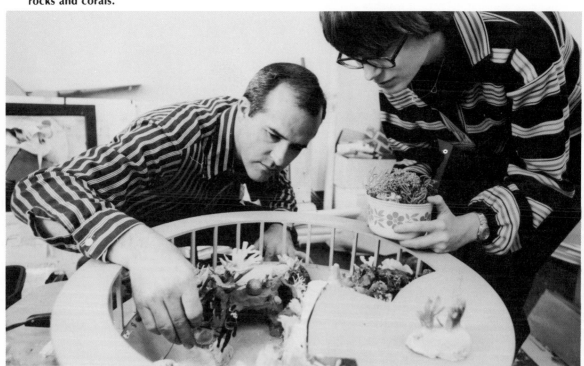

This is the actual Coral Reef exhibit. It contains 90,000 gallons or about 3,420,000 liters of water. Twice a day, crowds gather to watch the fish being fed by a diver who explains his work over a public address system.

It took several tries to produce the durable, safe, natural-looking artificial coral now used.

In some tanks, zibbets have found that a painted background solves two problems. In Chico's tank, soft greens control light and suggest his river-bottom home.

When there are major changes to be made and a whole section or gallery is to be redesigned, contractors, and aquarium engineers handle the construction. Heavy sheets of glass have to be sealed in place. Each tank is calked to make it leakproof. Changes in lighting and plumbing are made if these are needed.

After all this work is done, the people from the Exhibits Department or the aquarists from the Fishes Department install the habitat settings.

At the Shedd Aquarium, the aquarists take the responsibility for decorating many of the tanks, using natural materials. Zibbets concentrate on habitat settings assembled from manufactured materials.

Labels and informational signs to help visitors identify and learn about the fish are installed. The graphics are produced by the Education Department. Finally, the fish, which have all this time been kept in holding tanks, are put on public view.

So, when a parent points out a trout or salmon and promises a family fishing trip or when children laugh at minnows and turtles, aquarium workers feel they've been successful. An exhibit such as the "Fish of Lake Michigan" is worth all the effort and skill it required.

31

The Workers

■■■

An aquarium is a special place to work. The men and women there need many skills, plenty of curiosity and enthusiasm, and the willingness to work and share together.

What you don't see

Only about a third of an aquarium is seen by visitors, and perhaps that's too bad. A great deal of interesting work goes on all of the time, out of sight.

No two aquariums or oceanariums are the same in plan, nor are they just alike in operation.

City aquariums are built for people to enjoy and as places for study. They are supported by money gifts, memberships, admission fees, and taxes. Many oceanariums and some aquariums are run as businesses. They, too, offer research as well as entertainment.

The Shedd Aquarium was built as a gift to the city where it stands. By now you have found out something about how its collection is chosen and housed. But an aquarium is more than fish—it's men and women busy at many kinds of work.

The director knows fish—and people

The Shedd Aquarium employs about 75 workers, headed by the director, William Braker. He is a marine scientist, but he has to be a good leader and businessman, too. He is in charge of all that goes on: the exhibits, the workers, the educational programs, the spending decisions, and, often, the collecting expeditions.

On few jobs can one person be concerned with a sea catfish spawning, health requirements for divers, and leading travelers interested in zoology to the Galapagos Islands in the Pacific, west of Ecuador, to meet the strange

← **Pet a shark? That's what the diver in the Shedd Aquarium, Coral Reef exhibit is doing. This is a nurse shark, about 5½ feet long.**

33

wildlife found there. Each of these tasks is in one way or another typical of what makes a director's duties anything but dull.

Mr. Braker's worldwide reputation in his field brings him other experiences, too, such as serving as a consultant for the Iranian government when special environmental exhibits were being planned.

Of course the director doesn't clean out tanks, although he may pet Chico. He doesn't check the control panel which tells that all of the water system is operating, but he does hear about leaks.

The director is responsible for the smooth running of the whole aquarium and its staff. He has an assistant director to help him. The staff is divided into departments, each with its own head, called a curator, chief, or co-ordinator.

Departments and workers

How work is organized differs from one aquarium and oceanarium to another. But the same kind of work in general goes on even though department names and workers' titles may be different. At the Shedd Aquarium, the departments are listed in alphabetical order: Business, Education, Exhibits, Fishes, Maintenance, and Public Relations, which includes Membership. Each department is important, and together they make the aquarium successful.

Workers in some of the departments are now familiar to you. You have met, for example, the chief engineer and his crew who belong to the Maintenance Department. They are responsible for the aquarium's water, heating, cooling, and electrical systems. Building changes and repairs often involve their work.

The designers and creative men and women in the Exhibits Department are familiar, too. You know how they plan displays and work with the aquarists in the Fishes Department.

Workers carefully fit the thick glass panel in place. It will be the front wall of the exhibit tank, through which visitors will view the fish.

You've read about aquarists on collecting trips and special aquarists, like Chico's friend. Now it's time to look closely at some of the other work which goes on in the Fishes Department.

Fishes and aquarists

Suppose you could interview a fish swimming in the Coral Reef exhibit. Who would that fish say were the most important people at the aquarium? The aquarists who bring food, of course.

Aquarists belong to the Fishes Department. They work under the direction of a curator and an assistant curator. They almost always have one thing in common. When they were young they kept fish as pets and were curious about what they did.

Everyone in this department swims and dives. Being physically strong is important, too, because much of the equipment and some of the specimens are heavy and hard to move.

The aquarists' work area is bright and sunny, far different from the shadowy visitors' galleries with their windowlike views of fish swimming in their tanks. These tanks are open at the top, but the water level keeps visitors from watching aquarists at their work.

Behind the exhibit tanks are rows of holding tanks which look rather like large, open concrete tubs. Fish swim in some of these water-filled tanks.

Red signs dangle above tanks to re-

How to use artificial material for a display is discussed by Assistant Curator of Exhibits Jim Hemingway and designer Marc Fleischmann.

mind everyone to keep hands out of water—a hungry fish might just take a nip of a finger.

Holding tanks are like hospital rooms and hotel rooms—places where fish are isolated if they appear sick or kept waiting until they are ready to be put on display.

Aquarists are each responsible for certain fish, mammals, birds, turtles, or other sea life. They're often helped by volunteers. Some of the volunteers are young people who are interested in a career in biology or zoology.

Whether a fish is large or tiny, whether it has a short or long life span, an aquarist learns a great deal about its habits. He works hard to keep the fish healthy and active.

Some aquarists have the chance to work for a long time with some of their charges. The same aquarist for years looked after Chico, taking over his care on the day he arrived. Chico and his aquarist know each other well—you might be right in calling the man and dolphin good friends.

Special assignments

The Department of Fishes is headed by a curator and an assistant curator. Both are men with college degrees in biology and other subjects related to their work.

The curator is especially concerned with questions about the collection: how it should be expanded, how care can be improved, what changes should be made. The assistant curator has duties of his own. He tests water, does autopsies on dead fish, and knows what different aquarists are doing.

Some aquarists become specialists. For example, there are the aquarists who take care of the balanced aquariums, each a miniature habitat filled with shimmering color. Brilliant tropi-

An autopsy on a Russian sturgeon calls for cooperation between the Shedd Aquarium staff and that of the neighboring Field Museum of Natural History. Volunteers look on.

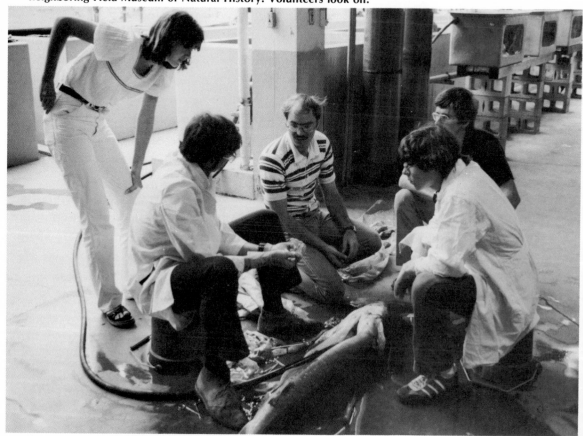

Aquarist Bill Gwozdz is responsible for beautiful small displays which contain a balance of tropical animals and plant life.

cal fish flash in and out among graceful water plants. The balance between fish and plants is important, and the aquarists watch for any signal of trouble.

A number of aquarists and sometimes a volunteer take turns being the diver who hand-feeds the fish and other creatures in the big Coral Reef tank. The divers know what different fish prefer and when it's necessary to coax a fish or an eel to eat.

The diver wears a mask fitted with a microphone. While swimming, the aquarist talks to the audience watching through the tank's glass windows. It's interesting to learn that fish of different kinds don't swim at random together. Some like the middle levels of the tank, others choose to stay close to the sandy floor. The diver points out fish which swim in schools and those that stay strictly alone.

Unexpected things sometimes happen in the big tank. When the sawfish was first put in the exhibit, it was small— but as time passed, it grew considerably. Once-playful pushes at the diver became painful encounters to avoid. Nipped fingers are another hazard to guard against. But the nurse sharks, floating lazily at the bottom of the tank, are nearly harmless and even friendly.

Care and feeding

When new fishes or other sea life arrive at the aquarium, they do not immediately join those already used to life in an aquarium tank.

The arrivals are kept by aquarists in an isolation holding tank. They are fed and watched for two or three weeks.

Aquarists look for signs of disease which may be fatal to a new fish or spread to healthy fish. They check for parasites, some of which may be harmful.

To live in their new home, fish will have to accept unfamiliar food. The eating habits they once had are not always useful in the aquarium. Fish cannot swim about, gulping smaller fish for a meal, nor can they scavenge freely for food left after some larger fish has eaten its fill.

Aquarists learn that fish eat in many ways. The paddlefish, a freshwater fish from the United States, gets its food by straining water through its mouth. The sturgeons have mouths that might re-

Fish, shrimp, squid, and a prepared food called trout pellets are items on the regular menu for aquarium diners.

Some specimens require individual feeding. Twice a week aquarist Rob Mottice feeds a shrimp mixture through a tube and bulb device to cold saltwater anemones.

mind you of a vacuum cleaner as they suck in food.

If a fish is a problem eater, an aquarist may try to tempt it to eat.

An octopus sometimes takes food from the aquarist's hand. It wraps its tentacles around the arm of the aquarist and holds on tightly as it feeds. Anemones, however, have to be fed by force.

When the piranhas are hungry, they eat in what is called a "feeding frenzy." They rush about madly, trying to eat anything and everything in their way, even each other.

Preparing food is part of the aquarists' work. Large orders of frozen seafood are trucked to the aquarium each week. Much of this is the same kind and quality of seafood sold to restaurants and markets: smelts, mackerel, herring, sardines, squids, jacks, and shrimp.

There are special items you'd probably not like to try: brine shrimp, horse heart, tubifex worms, dry food like that fed to goldfish in home tanks, and trout pellets. The pellets are made from cereals, fish meal, with added vitamins and minerals.

What's happening to the shark on this and the facing page? Above: Aquarist Mike Rigsby measures the exact amount of anesthetic to be given to the shark. At the left: Mike helps Assistant Curator of Fishes Roger Klocek lift the anesthetized shark out of its tank.

Frozen supplies are kept in freezers. Fish is thawed as needed, waste parts are cut away, and shrimp are peeled. Often this is enough preparation. But for some more choosy aquarium residents, food is combined and ground.

A new diet may be substituted in an effort to keep a fish from starving itself to death.

Health is important

Curators and aquarists want to keep fish healthy. Fish have diseases. They can be injured—bitten by other fish, scraped or cut on rocks or coral, or bruised by bumping into the sides of a tank.

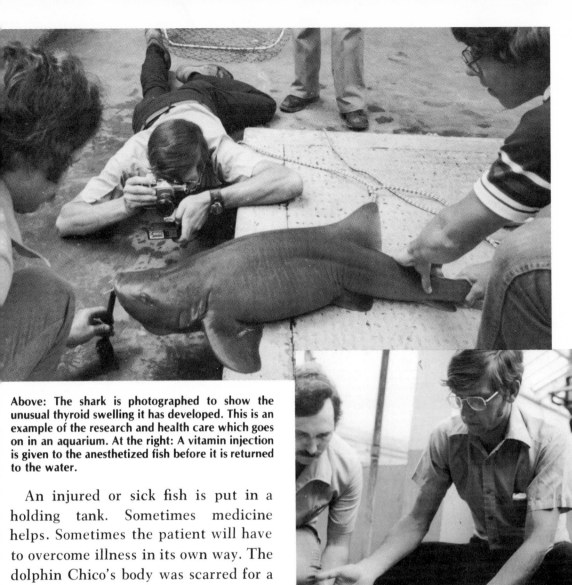

Above: The shark is photographed to show the unusual thyroid swelling it has developed. This is an example of the research and health care which goes on in an aquarium. At the right: A vitamin injection is given to the anesthetized fish before it is returned to the water.

An injured or sick fish is put in a holding tank. Sometimes medicine helps. Sometimes the patient will have to overcome illness in its own way. The dolphin Chico's body was scarred for a long time as the result of infections. There was no way to hurry the healing process.

When the 450-pound jewfish named Joshua was given an antibiotic injection, a fish scale was knocked loose. Studying it, the assistant curator counted 38 annual growth rings, the probable age of the giant fish.

41

Aquarists look after health needs when they make sure water temperatures are right and water is just as salty or fresh as it should be. Enough oxygen in the water is absolutely essential.

Housekeeping is important. Scavenger sea life will do some of this, eating the green algae which grow so rapidly on tank walls and glass fronts. Most tanks, though, need cleaning. From time to time displays are taken apart, scrubbed, and renewed.

Pumps, filters, and heaters must be checked. But fish care is different from human care in one way that helps aquarists. All fish do not have to be fed daily. Some get food twice a week, some even less often.

Contributing to science

An aquarium or an oceanarium is really a laboratory on a large scale for animal and plant study. Curators and aquarists observe water life closely, often through all or much of an individual specimen's life.

Research of different kinds often goes on. Breeding is especially important, but to breed and raise young in an artificial setting is difficult. This is partly because scientists still know so little about necessary conditions. No one understands as yet why horseshoe crabs choose only certain beaches for breeding grounds—and this is only one of many mysteries.

High school students use microscopes and laboratory equipment at the Shedd Aquatic Science Center. They are guided by Assistant Curator of Education Linda Wilson.

When the sea catfish at the Shedd Aquarium had live young, it was a notable occasion and won the aquarium a scientific award. Trying to breed endangered species has, however, often ended in failure.

Finding out why a fish has died may give a clue to care for living fish. An examination, or autopsy, provides information.

Aquariums contribute to science in other ways, too. They supply research workers with special materials. Carp, for instance, were given by the Shedd Aquarium to a university hospital to use in cardiac (heart) studies. At the New York Aquarium, the Osborne Laboratory has been studying horseshoe crabs in the course of cancer research.

Scientists sometimes visit the aquarium to observe and experiment. A behavioral engineer came to Chicago to set up an experiment with Chico. The dolphin was trained to react to light signals and hand signals. He learned to turn on lights in a certain order and to do underwater loops and tail stands. An extra bonus for Chico was the exercise and interest these activities added to his daily life. The scientist went away with useful observations to report.

Microscopes, films, and books

A laboratory with microscopes, study tanks, and all kinds of equipment—who uses it? Programs with titles like "From Seahorses to Sharks," "Food from the

Using visual aids, Rozell Willis, the volunteer coordinator in education, leads a study group in the Science Center.

The aquarium library is an inviting place to seek information on sea life and related careers.

Sea," and "No Bones About Them"—who will enjoy these? And who takes part in workshops in seashore biology and lakeshore biology or possibly joins a collecting trip?

The answer could be *you* if you live near the Shedd Aquarium or another aquarium where experiences like these are available to girls and boys and, in fact, to people of any age.

The Curator of Education heads a staff that includes teachers, a librarian, and volunteers. During the school year, class groups take part in programs planned for different ages. In the summer, there are story hours for youngsters in the library and programs in a room where models can be examined and films seen. Lectures and laboratory work are scheduled for high school students who will take a field trip to Florida.

Ramps make it easy for wheelchair students to get around. Models and dried specimens which can be handled help blind girls and boys learn about fish.

The comfortable, bright library has books as easy as picture books and as advanced as staff members need for research. There are books on marine mammals, plankton, sharks, pollution, law, aquaculture, and fish identification. There's career information, too.

During the first year after the Shedd Aquatic Science Center—where the laboratories, lecture rooms, and library are located—was open, more than 8,000 students took part in programs.

Some day, the education staff will probably be able to say with pride that a young person they helped in their laboratories and classes has become a scientist who is making valuable discoveries.

Adults, too, are served by the Education Department. Men and women of all ages become members of the aquarium and take an eight-week training course for volunteers. Some act as gallery guides, tankmen, divers, and assistants to the librarian. The aquarium people wonder how they ever got along without volunteers.

Making the aquarium known

It's newstime on TV, and there's a feature about the sharks at the city's aquarium. The reporter, in wet suit and goggles, gets into a tank with a nurse shark—and pets it!

If you see a program like that, it makes you want to look at that shark, even if you don't expect to let it touch your hand.

Newspaper articles describe new exhibits and tell about collecting trips and gifts. Perhaps there's an interview with an outstanding girl biology student who has been a diver in the Coral Reef tank.

Maybe a film is made where the star is a bottle-nosed dolphin or a whale at an oceanarium. Research articles get attention—they're written by aquarium people.

All these are ways that bring visitors to see fish and sea life on exhibit. It's fun and exciting, and it's a learning experience, too.

The Public Relations Department and its co-ordinator have a lot to do with letting reporters, TV newspeople, and others know when there's a newsworthy happening connected with the aquarium. A suggestion for a children's TV program can be welcome. The story of the opening of a new gallery is a reason to send photographers for a report.

Attracting visitors is certainly important; getting them really involved is even more important.

Checking films for a brochure is part of Kris Hansen's work as an assistant in Public Relations.

Like museums and zoological societies, aquariums often have membership programs. The fees members pay help support exhibits and research. Members share enthusiasm and take part in learning what happens in areas where visitors usually don't go. They meet the staff, and perhaps they volunteer their own skills where they're needed.

Still other workers

It's probably more exciting to feed piranhas or tag a big sea turtle for its release in the ocean, but it's necessary to have someone handle the business matters of the aquarium. An annual budget must be made out, bills paid, and contracts for work written. There's a great deal more, for an aquarium needs millions of dollars to operate.

The Business Department is involved in all of this work. Its staff includes office workers such as receptionists, secretaries, and bookkeepers.

Other people have assignments, too. Guards at entrances take admission tickets and give directions. At the gift shop, the manager makes sure there are all kinds of items for sale—books, shells, coral, models, and even T-shirts and caps. The profits from the shop support aquarium activities.

An aquarium is more than fish

At the bottom of this page is the symbol the Shedd Aquarium uses to identify itself.

On your first look, did you see the wave or the fish? Strangely enough, you cannot see both at the same time. And does the circle suggest our Earth with its oceans to you?

This symbol says what aquariums are about, not just the Shedd, but all aquariums and oceanariums. Showing how beautiful and entertaining fish can be is part of the purpose. Study and education are other purposes. But perhaps the main reason for an aquarium is to help you see how the worlds of air and water are related to each other, and how you depend upon both. The aquarium shows how our lives can be richer because we respect nature, and, for certain young people, it can be the beginning of a rewarding career.

Yes, an aquarium is far more than fish.

Glossary

aerate, to supply air and oxygen to water.

anemone (a nem′a nee), sea animal without a backbone that looks like a flower.

annual growth rings, bands on a fish scale that mark a year's growth.

aquarist, worker who cares for plant and animal life in an aquarium, a keeper.

aquarium, man-made environment in which live water plants and animals are exhibited.

autopsy, examination of a body after death, often to learn the cause of death.

biology, the science that deals with living things, both plants and animals.

cichlid (sik′lid), small tropical freshwater fish.

coral reef, rocklike formation in the sea, made up in part of skeletons of certain marine animals.

curator, manager or head of department, as Curator of Fishes.

endangered species, species that must be protected or it will die out.

fish, cold-blooded water animal with a backbone, fins, and gills.

food chain, how plants and animals are linked together as sources of food.

fresh water, body of water without salt, for example a river or inland lake.

Galapagos Islands (Ga lop′e gus), Pacific Ocean islands off South America.

gill, organ used by fish to obtain oxygen from water.

habitat, place where a plant or animal is naturally found.

isolation, being kept apart or alone.

larva, immature form of fish that is unlike the adult.

mammal, animal with a backbone, whose young is fed milk, and whose body is more or less covered with hair.

marine, having to do with the sea.

mollusk, animal without a backbone, having a soft body, often protected by a shell.

oceanarium, large saltwater aquarium.

parasite, organism that lives on another living organism, as fleas on a dog.

piranha (pi ron′ya), tropical freshwater fish with sharp teeth.

plankton, almost microscopic plants and animals that come together and float in water.

reptile, air-breathing animal with backbone and a body usually covered with scales.

reservoir, tank used to store water.

scavenger, animal that eats dead or decaying animal or plant life.

spawn, to produce or deposit eggs.

species, in plant or animal classification, a group that can interbreed with others of the same species.

specimen, sample typical of its kind, chosen for study or display.

zoology, branch of biology that deals with animals.

Index

algae, 42
aquarists, 5, 6, 7, 12, 13, 35–42
aquariums
  collections, 9–11, 27, 36
  departments, 34–35
  donations, 18
  history, 8–9, 17, 18, 24
  purpose, 6–7, 46
  See also oceanariums
Australian lungfish, 20
autopsies, 36, 42
breeding, 11, 20, 25, 42
Business Department, 46
carp, 8, 18, 43
Chico (freshwater dolphin), 5–6, 31, 36, 41, 43
cichlids, 25
clownfish, 23
collecting expeditions, 11–17
coral, 14, 30
curators, 12, 34, 36–42, 44
directors, 11–12, 16, 33–34
divers, 12, 14–16, 37, 45
dolphins, 5–6
  See also Chico
Education Department, 31, 34, 43–45
eels, 28
endangered species, 18, 20–21, 42
Exhibits Department, 27–31, 34
Fish and Wildlife Service, 18
Fishes Department, 31, 34, 35–40
  See also aquarists
food, 38–40
food chain, 16–17
health care, 35, 38–39, 40–42

horseshoe crabs, 42, 43
jewfish, 29, 41
John G. Shedd Aquarium
  See Shedd Aquarium
lion fish, 23
Maintenance Department, 24–26, 34
Marineland of Florida, 9
Marineland of the Pacific, 9, 27
National Aquarium, 8
New England Aquarium, 9
New York Aquarium, 9, 43
oceanariums, 6, 7, 9, 26–27
octopuses, 14, 39
paddlefish, 38
penguins, 10, 20–21
piranhas, 25, 39
plankton, 16
Public Relations Department, 45–46
research, 42–43
sawfish, 37
sea anemones, 10, 23, 39
sea catfish, 42
Sea World, 9
Seaquarium, 9, 19–20
sharks, 10, 12, 15, 18, 45
Shedd Aquarium (John G. Shedd Aquarium), 5–6, 9, 15–17, 20–21, 24–25, 26, 29, 33–34, 42–42, 44, 46
Shedd Aquatic Science Center, 44
Steinhart Aquarium, 9
threatened species, 20
turtles, 18, 19–20, 21
volunteers, 35, 44–45
water systems, 12, 23–26
whales, 6, 11